Egyptian Mythology

A Collection of the Best Egyptian Myths

Jason Dodd

Table of Contents

Introduction

Welcome to "Egyptian Mythology: A Collection of the Best Egyptian Myths," a journey through the timeless legends and tales that have shaped and defined one of the world's most fascinating ancient civilizations. In these pages, you will embark on a voyage through the mystical world of Egyptian deities, mythical creatures, and epic narratives that have captivated scholars, historians, and enthusiasts for centuries.

Chapter 1, "Gods & Goddesses," delves into the pantheon of Egyptian divinities, each with their unique roles, lineage, and reputations. From the sun god Ra, whose daily journey across the sky and through the underworld signifies the cycle of life and death, to Isis, the goddess of magic and motherhood, whose wisdom and protective nature resonate through several myths, this chapter is an exploration of divine power and influence.

In Chapter 2, "Other Characters," we move beyond the gods and goddesses to explore other significant entities in Egyptian mythology. The enigmatic Sphinx, and the formidable serpent Apep, the embodiment of chaos, are among the characters that add depth and complexity to these ancient stories.

The subsequent chapters are dedicated to the myths themselves, each a narrative rich in symbolism and cultural significance. Chapter 3, "Egyptian Creation Myths," explores the various accounts of how the world came to be, from the waters of Nun to the creative actions of Ptah. Chapter 4, "Osiris and Set," delves into the tale of betrayal and redemption within one of the most powerful divine families.

"The Contendings of Horus and Set," in Chapter 5, continues this family saga, detailing the struggle for power and legitimacy. Chapter 6, "Ra's Journey Through the Underworld," takes you on a nightly voyage filled with danger and the constant battle against chaos.

In Chapter 7, "The Tale of Two Brothers," a story of loyalty, betrayal, and magical transformations unfolds. Chapter 8, "Isis and the Seven Scorpions," highlights the protective and nurturing aspects of one of Egypt's most revered goddesses. Finally, Chapter 9, "Sekhmet and the Destruction of Mankind," presents a tale of wrath, compassion, and the duality of the gods.

"Egyptian Mythology: A Collection of the Best Egyptian Myths" is more than just a book; it's a portal to a world that has long since passed but continues to live in these age-old stories. Each chapter invites you to immerse yourself in the rich tapestry of Egyptian mythology, offering a glimpse into the beliefs, values, and imaginations of an ancient civilization whose legacy continues to enchant and inspire.

Chapter 1: Gods & Goddesses

Egyptian Mythology is home to a variety of different Gods and Goddesses, each with their own unique lineage, attributes, and roles. In this opening chapter, we'll introduce you to the many fascinating deities that are present within the ancient Egyptian myths.

Ra (Re)

Ra (also spelled Re) is one of the most significant and revered deities in ancient Egyptian mythology, embodying the sun and its life-giving power. As the sun god, Ra was seen as the ruler of all that he created and the father of all gods, humans, and creatures. His daily journey across the sky in his solar boat was symbolic of life's cycle, encompassing birth, death, and rebirth. In the morning, Ra was believed to be reborn in the form of the rising sun, symbolizing renewal and growth. As the sun set, he was thought to die and journey through the underworld, only to be reborn the next day.

Ra's role in the mythology is central and multifaceted. He was not only the king of the gods and the bringer of light but also a creator god. In many myths, he is described as having created the world and everything in it, either by his thoughts, words, or by his tears. Ra's eye was an extension of his power, often personified as the goddesses Hathor, Sekhmet, or Bastet. These goddesses executed his will, particularly in terms of vengeance and protection.

Ra's importance in Egyptian religion is evident in the way other gods were often linked or merged with him. For example, Amun, a chief deity of Thebes, was combined with Ra to form Amun-Ra, a powerful composite deity who absorbed characteristics of both gods. Similarly, Atum, the god of creation in the Heliopolitan creation myth, was also identified with Ra.

The myth of Ra's journey through the underworld is particularly significant. Each night, Ra was believed to travel through the Duat (underworld), overcoming obstacles and battling the serpent Apophis, a symbol of chaos and destruction. This journey was not just a battle for Ra's survival but for the maintenance of the cosmic order and the cycle of day and night.

In art and iconography, Ra is often depicted as a man with a falcon head, crowned with a solar disk encircled by a cobra (uraeus), symbolizing his royal status, power, and connection to the divine. Temples dedicated to Ra, such as the sun temples, were centers of worship and ritual, emphasizing his immense influence in Egyptian culture and religion. Ra's cult was so influential that the Pharaohs, considered the sons of Ra, aligned themselves closely with him to reinforce their divine right to rule.

Osiris

Osiris is a central figure in Egyptian mythology, known primarily as the god of the afterlife, the underworld, and the dead, but he is also associated with life, fertility, and vegetation. He is often depicted as a mummified king, embodying the concept of resurrection and eternal life. Osiris's story and symbolism deeply influenced Egyptian religious beliefs and practices, especially regarding death and the afterlife.

The cult of Osiris had a significant impact on Egyptian society. It led to the development of various religious practices, including the concept of divine kingship, where Pharaohs were seen as earthly embodiments of Osiris. In death, the Pharaohs, like Osiris, were mummified and expected to rule in the afterlife. It was believed that the deceased would be judged by Osiris in the Hall of Ma'at, where their heart would be weighed against the feather of truth.

In art, Osiris is typically depicted as a mummified king, holding the crook and flail, symbols of royal authority, and wearing the Atef crown, a tall, white headdress with feathers on either side. His story, particularly of his resurrection, was central to Egyptian religion and had a lasting influence on the development of funerary customs and beliefs about the afterlife.

Isis

Isis is one of the most important and complex goddesses in ancient Egyptian mythology, revered for her myriad roles and attributes. She is known primarily as a goddess of magic, motherhood, fertility, and as a protector of the dead. Isis's versatility in the Egyptian pantheon is reflected in her various titles and roles, ranging from the mother of the pharaoh to a symbol of divine protection.

In mythology, Isis is most famously known through the myth of Osiris, her husband, who was murdered by his brother Set. Isis's role extends beyond this myth. She is also considered the ideal mother and wife; her relationship with Osiris and Horus served as a moral standard for all women in Egypt. As a mother, she is often depicted nursing Horus, symbolizing the royal lineage and the protection she provides. Her magical abilities, showcased in various myths, made her a goddess of healing and a protector against evil forces, and she was often invoked in spells for protection and health.

In addition to her religious roles, Isis was a central figure in Egyptian state and popular religion. She was worshipped by pharaohs and common people alike, with temples dedicated to her throughout Egypt and the wider Mediterranean world. Her worship even extended beyond the boundaries of Egypt, with temples and devotees in places like Greece and Rome.

Isis's iconography often depicts her with a throne-shaped headdress, representing her role as the mother of Horus, who was often considered the living king or pharaoh. She is also shown with wings, symbolizing her role as a protector, or holding an ankh, the symbol of life.

Horus

Horus is a pivotal deity in ancient Egyptian mythology, known primarily as the god of the sky, kingship, and protection. He is often depicted as a falcon or as a man with the head of a falcon. The cult of Horus is one of the oldest in Egypt, and his role and symbolism evolved significantly over time, reflecting the changes in religious and political thought in ancient Egyptian society.

One of the most central aspects of Horus's mythology is his association with the Pharaoh. Horus was believed to be the divine protector of the ruler of Egypt, and each Pharaoh was considered to be the living embodiment of Horus. This connection established the Pharaoh's divine right to rule and linked the stability and prosperity of the country directly to Horus's power and favor.

The most famous myth involving Horus is his conflict with Set, the god of chaos, desert, and disorder. This conflict, known as the Contendings of Horus and Set, is a foundational myth in Egyptian mythology. This myth is covered in detail in chapter 5.

Horus's role extended beyond the political realm. As a sky god, he was also seen as the god of the sun and moon, with his right eye representing the sun and his left eye the moon. The myth of Horus's lost eye, in which Set damages or steals one of his eyes, and the subsequent healing of the eye, symbolizes the phases of the moon and the restoration of wholeness and health. The Eye of Horus, also known as the Wadjet, became a powerful symbol of protection and healing, used extensively in amulets and other forms of protective art.

In terms of worship, Horus had many temples across Egypt, and his cult was particularly prominent in the city of Edfu, home to a large and well-preserved temple dedicated to him. The worship of Horus spanned the entirety of ancient Egyptian history, reflecting his enduring significance as a symbol of kingship, protection, and the triumph of order over chaos.

Set (Seth)

Set (also spelled Seth) is a complex and multifaceted deity in ancient Egyptian mythology, often associated with chaos, storms, deserts, and foreign lands. His role and perception in Egyptian mythology evolved over time, from a respected deity to a symbol of malevolence and chaos, reflecting the changing religious and political landscape of ancient Egypt.

In early Egyptian mythology, Set was a god of strength, storms, and foreign lands, and he was not always seen in a negative light. He was respected for his strength and was considered a protector of Ra, the sun god, during his nightly journey through the underworld. Set fought off the serpent Apophis, a force of chaos that threatened to devour Ra's solar barge and plunge the world into darkness. This protective role showcased Set's importance in maintaining cosmic order.

However, Set's image underwent significant changes, particularly due to his role in one of the most famous myths of Egyptian mythology: the murder of Osiris and the subsequent conflict with Horus, Osiris's son. In this myth, Set kills his brother Osiris out of jealousy and battles Horus, who seeks to avenge his father and reclaim the throne. Set's actions in this story paint him as the embodiment of envy, violence, and disorder, opposing the rightful order represented by Osiris and Horus. The myth symbolizes the eternal struggle between order and chaos, with Set often depicted as the usurper and antagonist.

Despite his negative portrayal in this and other myths, Set was not always seen as an evil figure. He had his temples and worshippers, particularly in regions where his more destructive aspects were revered or appeased. For example, his association with the desert and foreign lands meant that he was sometimes seen as a protector of caravans and distant travels.

In iconography, Set is often depicted as a creature not easily identified, known as the Set animal, a mythical beast with a curved snout, square ears, and a forked tail. This unique appearance further emphasized his role as a deity of the unusual and the foreign.

Anubis

Anubis is one of the most iconic and recognizable deities in ancient Egyptian mythology, often depicted as a man with the head of a jackal or as a jackal itself. His role in the pantheon is primarily associated with mummification, the afterlife, and the protection of graves and cemeteries.

The origin of Anubis is somewhat shrouded in mystery, but he is generally believed to have been a guardian and protector of the dead. He was originally the god of the underworld before this role was taken over by Osiris, after which Anubis's focus shifted more towards the embalming process and the care of the dead. He was seen as the one who guided souls into the afterlife, ensuring their safe passage and judging their hearts in the Weighing of the Heart ceremony, a crucial step in determining a soul's fate in the afterlife.

In the Weighing of the Heart, which is vividly depicted in the Book of the Dead, Anubis measures the heart of the deceased against Ma'at's feather of truth and justice. If the heart is found to be as light as the feather, the soul is deemed worthy to enter the paradise of the Field of Reeds. If the heart is heavier, laden with sin, it is devoured by Ammit, the soul-eating monster, resulting in the second death, a permanent end of existence.

Anubis's role as the protector of graves also made him a guardian against grave robbers and a guide for the dead. He was invoked to protect the sanctity of the tomb and the safety of the body and possessions within it, which were crucial for the deceased's journey and life in the afterlife.

Thoth

Thoth, also known as Djehuty or Tehuti in ancient Egyptian mythology, is a deity of immense significance and broad influence. He is often depicted as a man with the head of an ibis or as a baboon, both animals sacred to him. Thoth played a crucial role in many aspects of Egyptian mythology and religion, embodying wisdom, writing, magic, science, judgment, and the moon.

In mythology, Thoth was considered the heart and tongue of Ra, the sun god, acting as an intermediary between the will of the gods and the human world. This role highlights Thoth as a god of wisdom and knowledge, a divine communicator and counselor to both gods and humans. He was also the scribe of the gods, credited with the invention of writing and hieroglyphs, which was essential for maintaining the cosmos, recording history, and performing religious rites.

Thoth was also associated with the moon and time. His connection with lunar cycles led to his portrayal as a god of reckoning time and the inventor of the calendar. The lunar association gave Thoth a role in regulating the heavens and maintaining the universe's balance. He was believed to be self-created, a notion that further enhanced his image as a god of creation, knowledge, and magic.

In addition to his significant roles in mythology, Thoth was widely venerated across Egypt, with the town of Hermopolis as his major cult center. His worship often involved aspects of science and knowledge, with scribes and scholars particularly revering him. The Greeks, recognizing his attributes of wisdom and learning, identified Thoth with their god Hermes, creating the composite deity Hermes Trismegistus, who became associated with alchemy and occult wisdom.

Hathor

Hathor, one of the most beloved and multifaceted deities in ancient Egyptian mythology, is often depicted as a cow, a woman with the head of a cow, or a woman wearing a headdress of cow horns and a solar disk. She embodies a wide range of roles and attributes, including love, beauty, music, motherhood, fertility, and joy. Hathor is also associated with the sky, the sun, and the afterlife, making her one of the most versatile and widely venerated deities in the Egyptian pantheon.

One of Hathor's most significant roles was as a goddess of love, beauty, and sexuality, akin to Aphrodite or Venus in Greek and Roman mythology. She was invoked in matters of love and was a patroness of music and dance, which were essential components of worship in her temples. Her joyful and benevolent nature was celebrated in festivals, notably the Feast of Hathor, where music, dance, and merriment were part of the rituals to honor her.

Despite her generally benign nature, Hathor had a fearsome aspect as well. In one myth, she becomes Sekhmet, a lioness goddess, to enact revenge on humanity for its disobedience. However, Ra prevents her from destroying all humanity, and she reverts to her gentle form as Hathor, illustrating the dual nature of the divine.

Hathor's worship was widespread, with her primary cult center at Dendera, where her grand temple still stands today. Her cult also had a significant influence on the role and status of women and priestesses in ancient Egyptian society. Hathor's enduring popularity throughout the history of Egypt is a testament to her complex and embracing nature, encompassing both the nurturing and the destructive forces of life.

Sobek

Sobek, revered in ancient Egyptian mythology, is a distinctive and powerful deity characterized by his crocodile form. He is often depicted as a man with a crocodile head or as a crocodile itself, embodying the fearsome and awe-inspiring aspects of these creatures. Sobek's role in Egyptian mythology is multifaceted, encompassing themes of fertility, strength, protection, and the might of the pharaoh.

Originating from the Old Kingdom, Sobek's worship initially centered around the Faiyum region and the Nile River, where crocodiles were abundant. As a creature of the Nile, Sobek was seen as a god of the river's fertility and its life-giving properties. His association with water also connected him to the creation and the primordial waters of Nun. Sobek was thus viewed as a creator deity in some traditions, involved in the creation of the world and the order of the universe.

In contrast to his aggressive characteristics, Sobek was also revered as a god of fertility and a source of life-giving water. This duality reflects the Egyptians' understanding of the natural world, where the Nile's dangerous creatures, like the crocodile, were also essential to the river's fertility and, by extension, the fertility of the land.

Throughout Egyptian history, Sobek's worship varied in intensity, with significant cult centers at Crocodilopolis (now

Medinet El-Faiyum) and Kom Ombo, where he was worshipped alongside Horus. The temple at Kom Ombo uniquely illustrates the duality of Sobek and Horus, juxtaposing the dangerous and protective aspects of Sobek with the healing and royal aspects of Horus.

Sekhmet

Sekhmet, a formidable and complex deity in ancient Egyptian mythology, is renowned for her dual nature of ferocity and healing. She is often depicted as a lioness or as a woman with the head of a lioness, embodying the aggressive power and strength of a lion, which was revered and feared in equal measure by the ancient Egyptians. Her name means "the powerful one," a fitting title for a goddess who personifies both destructive and protective forces.

Sekhmet's most notable myth involves her role as the avenger of the sun god Ra. According to the myth, when Ra grew old and humans conspired against him, he sent Sekhmet to punish humanity. This myth is recounted in Chapter 9.

Aside from her wrathful aspect, Sekhmet was also revered as a goddess of healing and medicine. The Egyptians believed that her powers of destruction could also be turned to protect and heal. As such, she was often invoked by physicians and healers, and her priests were known for their skills in medicine. This dual role of Sekhmet underscores the Egyptian understanding of balance – where destruction and healing are two sides of the same coin.

In terms of worship, Sekhmet had a significant cult following, with one of her most important cult centers at Memphis. Here, she was worshipped alongside Ptah, the god of creation and craftsmanship, and Nefertum, the god of sunrise. Her temples often featured statues of the goddess, and her annual festival was a time of feasting and revelry.

Ptah

Ptah, a pivotal deity in ancient Egyptian mythology, is revered as the god of craftsmen, architects, and builders, and is closely associated with creation and the arts of civilization. He is often depicted as a mummified man, standing or seated, holding a staff that combines the symbols of life (ankh), stability (djed), and power (was scepter). This iconography underscores his role as a stabilizing and life-giving force in the universe.

In Egyptian cosmology, Ptah holds a unique position as a creator deity. In the Memphite Theology, an important religious and philosophical text, Ptah is exalted as the primeval creator god who brought the world into being through the power of his heart and speech. This concept is profound in Egyptian thought, where words and thoughts were considered tangible and potent forces.

Ptah's association with craftsmanship and building is not just symbolic but was integral to Egyptian society. He was considered the divine patron of artisans, sculptors, and builders, believed to imbue them with the skills and inspiration needed for their crafts.

Ptah's worship was centered in Memphis, one of ancient Egypt's most important cities, where he was part of a triad along with his consort Sekhmet, the lioness goddess of war and healing, and their son Nefertum, the god of the lotus blossom. This triad reflects a complete cycle of creation, destruction, and rebirth, encapsulating the fundamental aspects of the Egyptian understanding of the world.

Bastet (Bast)

Bastet, also known as Bast, is a multifaceted goddess in ancient Egyptian mythology, initially depicted as a lioness goddess but later more commonly as a domestic cat or a woman with the head of a cat or lioness. Her transformation from a fierce lioness to a benign cat goddess over time reflects the changing cultural and religious landscape of ancient Egypt.

In her earlier form as a lioness, Bastet was associated with the sun god Ra as his daughter and was a fierce protector of both the god and the land. This aspect emphasized her role as a goddess of warfare, paralleling the protective nature of the lioness. She was believed to wield fiery power against the enemies of Ra, acting as a defender of the sun god and by extension, the pharaoh and the nation.

However, as her cult evolved, Bastet's image softened from a fierce warrior deity to a protector of homes and domesticity. She became associated with fertility, childbirth, and motherhood, and was revered as a nurturing and protective figure. This gentler aspect likely emerged from her association with domesticated cats, which were valued in Egyptian society for their protective instincts against vermin and their nurturing nature as mothers.

The cult of Bastet was centered in the city of Bubastis in the Nile Delta, which became a major site of worship and pilgrimage. The city housed a grand temple dedicated to Bastet, renowned for its splendor. Her annual festival was one of the most joyous and popular in ancient Egypt, characterized by music, dancing, feasting, and river processions.

Nephthys

Nephthys, a significant yet enigmatic goddess in ancient Egyptian mythology, is often associated with mourning, the night, and protection. She is depicted as a woman with hieroglyphic signs on her head representing her name, which means "Lady of the House," thought to refer to the temple or the sky. Nephthys is the daughter of Nut, the sky goddess, and Geb, the earth god, and sister to Isis, Osiris, and Set.

Despite being married to Set, the god of chaos and disorder, Nephthys is not depicted as malevolent. Instead, she is seen as a loyal sister and a protective deity. Her relationship with Set is complex and often seen as symbolic of the balance between order and chaos, as she balances his destructive nature with her protective and nurturing qualities.

Nephthys also holds a connection to the night and darkness, contrasting and complementing her sister Isis, who is associated with the day. This duality between Nephthys and Isis reflects the dual nature of the world, encompassing both life and death, light and dark.

In Egyptian iconography and worship, Nephthys was often paired with Isis, and together they were depicted on coffins, amulets, and in temple reliefs. They were believed to flank the bier of the deceased, providing protection and ensuring a safe journey to the afterlife.

Amun (Amon, Ammon)

Amun, also known as Amon or Ammon, is a major deity in ancient Egyptian mythology, initially worshipped as a local Theban god. Over time, he rose to prominence and became one of the most important and powerful gods in the Egyptian pantheon, eventually being identified as the king of the gods. Amun's name means "the hidden one" or "the invisible," reflecting his mysterious nature and his role as a deity of unseen powers and mysteries.

Originally, Amun was a deity associated with the air and wind, an invisible force that mirrored his conceptual nature. However, his attributes and significance greatly expanded, especially after the Theban rulers of the New Kingdom elevated him to supreme status. This elevation was not only a religious but also a political maneuver, as Thebes became the capital of the unified Egypt.

The most significant transformation in Amun's worship came with his amalgamation with Ra, the sun god, forming Amun-Ra. This combination merged Amun's invisible aspects with Ra's visible power as the sun, creating a composite deity that embodied the essential elements of both gods. Amun-Ra was revered as the creator god, the source of all life, and the upholder of ma'at (the order and balance of the universe). He was considered both the father of the pharaohs and the protector of the poor and oppressed, encompassing universal aspects of power, justice, and benevolence.

Amun's worship reached its zenith during the New Kingdom, with the construction of the massive temple complex at Karnak, dedicated to Amun-Ra. This temple became the most important religious center in Egypt, where elaborate rituals and ceremonies were conducted, and vast offerings were made to secure the deity's favor.

In iconography, Amun is often depicted as a man wearing a tall, plumed headdress and holding a scepter, symbolizing his royal authority and divine nature. He is also sometimes shown with a ram's head or as a ram, representing fertility and creative power.

Ma'at

Ma'at in ancient Egyptian mythology is not just a goddess but also a concept that represents truth, balance, order, harmony, law, morality, and justice. She is the personification of the fundamental order of the universe, without which both cosmic and societal chaos would ensue. Unlike other deities, Ma'at is more of an abstract principle given a divine form, integral to the very fabric of existence in the ancient Egyptian worldview.

Ma'at, as a goddess, is often depicted as a woman wearing a feather upon her head, the Feather of Truth, which is central to the weighing of the heart ceremony in the afterlife. In this critical judgment process, the heart of the deceased is weighed against Ma'at's feather in the Hall of Ma'at. This ceremony, overseen by Osiris and recorded by Thoth, determined the moral righteousness of the deceased's soul. If the heart was lighter than the feather, the soul was deemed worthy of the afterlife; if heavier, it was devoured by the demon Ammit, representing the annihilation of the soul.

The concept of Ma'at pervaded all aspects of ancient Egyptian life and was fundamental to the functioning of society. Pharaohs were considered the chief upholders of Ma'at, responsible for maintaining cosmic and societal harmony. Their rule was legitimized by their ability to uphold Ma'at, and they were often shown in art making offerings of Ma'at to the gods, symbolizing their dedication to maintaining balance and order.

Nut

Nut is a prominent goddess in ancient Egyptian mythology, embodying the sky and heavens. She is often depicted as a star-covered woman arching over the earth, her body forming the vault of the sky, touching the horizons with her fingertips and toes. This vivid imagery represents Nut as a protective figure, covering and enveloping the world, separating the chaos of the cosmos from the ordered life on earth.

Nut's role in Egyptian mythology is multifaceted, deeply intertwined with the concepts of birth, death, and rebirth. As the sky goddess, she is the mother of the sun and the moon, which she swallows each evening and gives birth to each morning, symbolizing the daily cycle of sunset and sunrise, as well as the eternal cycle of time. This act also associates Nut with regeneration and renewal, as each day is seen as a rebirth and a new beginning.

In funerary beliefs, Nut played a crucial role as a protective deity. She was believed to shelter and protect the souls of the dead, guiding them into the afterlife. The inside of sarcophagi often depicted Nut with outstretched wings, symbolizing her role as a protector of the deceased in their journey. Additionally, various spells and texts, like the "Book of Nut," provided details of her heavenly domain, offering insight into the ancient Egyptians' views of the cosmos and the afterlife.

Geb

Geb is a pivotal deity in ancient Egyptian mythology, personifying the earth. He is often depicted as a man lying beneath the sky goddess Nut, his sister and wife, with the air god Shu standing between them to separate earth and sky. Geb's portrayal in this iconic image symbolizes the ancient Egyptian understanding of the world's physical structure, with Geb as the earth holding all living things in his embrace and Nut as the sky arched over him.

As the god of the earth, Geb had a crucial role in Egyptian cosmology and was associated with vegetation, agriculture, and the fertility of the land. He was believed to cause earthquakes and was sometimes depicted with vegetation growing from his body, emphasizing his connection to the earth's bounty. His laughter was said to cause earthquakes, which reflects the ancient Egyptians' attempts to explain natural phenomena through the actions of their gods.

Geb's lineage is significant in Egyptian mythology. He is one of the children of Shu, the god of air, and Tefnut, the goddess of moisture. Together with his sister Nut, Geb fathered some of the most important Egyptian deities: Osiris, Isis, Set, and Nephthys. This divine family forms a critical component of Egyptian mythological narratives, especially the famous Osiris myth, where Geb's children play central roles.

Geb's role as an earth deity also made him a symbol of kingship. The pharaoh was often referred to as "Heir of Geb," which emphasized the king's role as the earthly representative of the divine order and his responsibility to maintain ma'at (balance and harmony) in the land. This connection reinforced the idea that the pharaoh was the link between the divine and the earthly realms.

Khnum

Khnum, an ancient Egyptian deity with a significant role in mythology, is often depicted as a ram-headed god, symbolizing fertility and creative power. Originating from the earliest periods of Egyptian history, Khnum's cult was centered at Elephantine

Island near the First Cataract of the Nile, a region that was crucial for the annual flooding of the Nile, which was essential for agriculture.

Khnum's primary role in Egyptian mythology is as a god of the Nile's source and the inundation, the annual flooding that deposited rich silt along the riverbanks, enabling agriculture. He was believed to control the flow of the Nile's waters, and thus, he was revered as a god who brought fertility and life to the land. This connection with the Nile's life-giving waters also extended to his being seen as a creator god.

Khnum's worship did not reach the same heights as that of deities like Osiris or Ra, but he maintained a steady presence in Egyptian religion, especially in regions close to the Nile's cataracts. His temples, particularly on Elephantine Island, were important religious centers.

Tefnut

Tefnut, a deity in ancient Egyptian mythology, personifies moisture, specifically the concepts of dew and rain. She is an integral part of the Heliopolitan creation myth, representing one of the fundamental elements of the natural world. Tefnut is often depicted as a lioness or as a woman with the head of a lioness, signifying her connection to the fierce and powerful aspects of nature. In some representations, she is shown with a solar disk on her head, linking her to the sun god Ra.

As a goddess of moisture, Tefnut's role was crucial in maintaining the balance and order of the cosmos (Ma'at). She was responsible for the nourishing dew and rain, essential for agriculture and the survival of the people and the land. Her association with moisture also extended to the concept of fertility, as water was vital for the fertility of the land and the proliferation of life.

In Egyptian religious practices, Tefnut was worshipped as part of a pair with her brother Shu. They were often depicted together, symbolizing the interdependence of air and moisture. While Tefnut did not have a widespread individual cult, her role in the cosmic order was acknowledged in religious texts and temple inscriptions.

Shu

Shu is a significant deity in ancient Egyptian mythology, personifying the air and the atmosphere. As a primordial god, he plays a crucial role in the creation and maintenance of the world. Shu is often depicted as a man wearing an ostrich feather, or sometimes just the feather itself, which represents lightness and the air.

One of Shu's most vital roles in mythology is his act of separating the sky from the earth. He is often depicted holding up Nut, the sky goddess, away from her brother and husband Geb, the earth god. This separation created the space in which the mortal world exists, with Shu himself representing the atmosphere between earth and sky. This act is fundamental to the structured world the ancient Egyptians believed in, where the cosmic order was maintained by the separation of these primordial forces.

Shu's role as the god of air also involves him being seen as a calming and cooling influence, a force that brings balance and order. He was invoked for bringing fresh air and for the relief that a breeze brings in a hot climate. Additionally, as a deity associated with light and air, Shu was also connected with the principle of life and the sustenance of living creatures.

Despite his importance in mythology, Shu did not have a large cult following like some other Egyptian deities. However, his role in the creation and his function in maintaining the cosmic order made him an integral part of Egyptian religious beliefs. Temples and texts often refer to him in the context of creation and his function as a supporter of the sky, highlighting his significance in the Egyptian understanding of the world.

Neith

Neith is a complex and ancient deity in Egyptian mythology, revered as a goddess of war, hunting, creation, and weaving. Her worship dates back to the Predynastic period, making her one of the oldest deities in the Egyptian pantheon. Neith is often depicted as a woman wearing the Red Crown of Lower Egypt, with a bow and arrows across her shoulders, symbolizing her role as a warrior and huntress.

One of Neith's most significant aspects is her role as a creator goddess. In some creation myths, particularly those centered in the city of Sais in the Nile Delta, Neith is considered the primeval creator, a self-created deity who gave birth to the sun and thus initiated the cycle of life. This aspect of Neith as a mother and creator contrasts with her more martial attributes, showcasing her as a deity of dual and complementary nature. She was also regarded as the mother of Sobek, the crocodile god, emphasizing her role in the cycle of life and death.

In her capacity as a war goddess, Neith was invoked for protection in battle. Her fierce nature was highly respected, and she was believed to be an expert archer and a formidable opponent. This martial aspect made her a protector deity, particularly of the pharaoh and the Egyptian state. Her role as a protector extended to the dead in the afterlife, where she was believed to weave the shroud for the deceased, a connection to her association with weaving.

The worship of Neith was particularly prominent in the western Delta and the city of Sais, where a great temple was dedicated to her. Her cult was one of the most enduring in Egypt, with her practices and rituals evolving over the millennia but always retaining her core aspects of creation, protection, and duality.

Serqet (Selket)

Serqet (also spelled Selket, Selqet, or Selcis) is a significant goddess in ancient Egyptian mythology, primarily known as the deity of scorpions, healing, and protection against venomous stings and bites. Her role in the Egyptian pantheon is complex, encompassing aspects of protection, healing, and the afterlife.

Often depicted as a woman with a scorpion on her head or as a scorpion with a woman's head, Serqet's imagery directly associates her with the creatures she governs. In a land where scorpion stings were a common and dangerous occurrence, her worship was particularly important. She was invoked for her powers of protection against venomous animals and was believed to have control over these creatures.

Serqet's cult did not have the prominence or the extensive temple-building of some other Egyptian deities, but her role in everyday life and in funerary practices was significant. Her worship was more personal and domestic, involving amulets, spells, and small shrines, reflecting the immediate and practical nature of her protection.

Khepri

Khepri is a unique and significant deity in ancient Egyptian mythology, associated with the rising sun, creation, movement, and rebirth. He is often depicted as a scarab beetle or as a man with a scarab for a head. This imagery is deeply symbolic, deriving from the behavior of the scarab beetle, which rolls dung into a ball for its eggs, an action the Egyptians saw as a metaphor for the movement of the sun across the sky and the cycle of life and rebirth.

In Egyptian cosmology, Khepri represents the aspect of the sun god Ra as the rising sun, embodying the idea of renewal and rebirth each morning. The name "Khepri" itself is related to the Egyptian verb "kheper," meaning "to develop" or "to come into being." This notion directly connects Khepri to the theme of creation and transformation. He is often considered an aspect of the sun god Ra, who takes different forms as he travels through the sky: Khepri in the morning, Ra at noon, and Atum in the evening.

Khepri's association with the scarab beetle held significant symbolic importance in Egyptian culture. The scarab represented life, regeneration, and rebirth. Scarab amulets were common in ancient Egypt, worn for protection and as a symbol of the enduring human soul. These amulets were also placed over the heart of the deceased in mummification practices, ensuring safe passage and rebirth in the afterlife.

In art and iconography, Khepri was often depicted pushing the sun disk through the sky, mirroring the scarab beetle's behavior with its dung ball. This depiction underscores his role in the movement of the sun and the perpetuation of the cycle of life, death, and rebirth.

Mut

Mut, an important goddess in ancient Egyptian mythology, is revered as the mother goddess, embodying the concepts of motherhood, queenship, and the sky. Her name itself means "mother," reflecting her maternal role in the divine realm. Mut was worshipped as a primal deity, a creator goddess, and a protective figure, often depicted as a woman wearing a double crown or a vulture headdress, symbolizing her connection to royalty and her role as a divine mother.

Mut's significance in Egyptian religion grew over time, particularly during the New Kingdom, when she became part of the Theban triad with Amun, the king of the gods, and their son Khonsu, the moon god. This triad was central to Theban religious beliefs and practices. As the consort of Amun, Mut was worshipped as the queen of the gods, and her cult was closely tied to that of Amun, reflecting the close relationship between divine and earthly kingship. The temple complex at Karnak in Thebes became the center of her worship, where she had a significant temple and a sacred lake.

Mut's maternal aspect was not limited to the divine realm; she was also considered a mother to the pharaoh and, by extension, to the Egyptian people. She was often invoked for protection, particularly of women and children, and her protective nature extended to the afterlife, where she safeguarded the souls of the deceased.

Atum

Atum, one of the most ancient and significant deities in Egyptian mythology, is revered as a creator god and a symbol of completeness and totality. His name translates to "the complete one" or "the finisher," indicating his role as both the creator and the final destination in the cycle of life and death. Atum is often depicted as a man wearing the double crown of Upper and Lower Egypt, signifying his authority over the entire land.

In the Heliopolitan creation myth, one of the predominant cosmogonies in ancient Egyptian religion, Atum is the first god to emerge from the primordial waters of Nun, representing the chaos that existed before creation. Standing on the primeval mound, Atum began the process of creation through self-engendering. He spat out Shu, the god of air, and Tefnut, the goddess of moisture, thereby initiating the creation of the world and the other gods. This act of self-creation made Atum a symbol of the creative force in the universe, embodying the concept of self-generation and the cyclical nature of life.

Atum's role as a creator is not limited to the physical world; he is also responsible for creating the ka, the vital essence or spirit, in humans. This connection with the ka established Atum as a critical figure in the afterlife and the Egyptians' understanding of existence beyond death. In later myths, Atum was also seen as the setting sun, representing the cycle of the day and the passage of life, as opposed to Ra, who represented the rising sun and the creation of life.

In the later periods of Egyptian history, Atum's role evolved and merged with that of other deities, particularly Ra. In this syncretized form as Atum-Ra, he embodied the combined attributes of both gods, symbolizing the sun's cycle from dawn to dusk and the overarching creative force in the universe.

The worship of Atum was centered in Heliopolis (modern-day Cairo), where he was part of the Ennead, a group of nine deities that included Atum and his descendants. As the first god of the Ennead, Atum held a place of high reverence and was considered the father of the gods, the ultimate source from which all life originated.

The Four Sons of Horus

In Egyptian mythology, the Four Sons of Horus hold a significant role, particularly in funerary practices and beliefs about the afterlife. They are seen as protective deities, each guarding one of the four canopic jars, which contained the embalmed internal organs of the deceased. Each son was associated with a specific compass point and a particular internal organ.

Imsety: Often depicted as a human-headed god, Imsety was responsible for guarding the liver. He was associated with the south and was under the protection of the goddess Isis.

Hapi: Represented with the head of a baboon, Hapi protected the lungs. He was associated with the north and was under the protection of the goddess Nephthys.

Duamutef: With the head of a jackal, Duamutef was the guardian of the stomach. He was linked with the east and was under the protection of the goddess Neith.

Qebehsenuef: Depicted with the head of a falcon, Qebehsenuef guarded the intestines. He was associated with the west and was under the protection of the goddess Serqet (Selket).

The Four Sons of Horus were not just guardians of physical organs; they also had a spiritual role. They were believed to help protect and sustain the soul of the deceased in the afterlife. The organs preserved in the canopic jars were essential for the deceased's survival in the afterlife, and thus the protection afforded by these deities was considered crucial.

The prominence of the Four Sons of Horus in Egyptian funerary culture is evident from the prevalence of their depictions on canopic jars, coffins, and tomb walls. Their role reflects the ancient Egyptians' beliefs in the importance of physical preservation and spiritual protection in achieving a successful journey to the afterlife. This combination of physical and spiritual elements in the funerary practices highlights the complex nature of Egyptian religious beliefs and their focus on the afterlife.

Tawaret

Tawaret, in Egyptian mythology, is a goddess who played a crucial role as a protector of women during pregnancy and childbirth. Her name, which means "She Who is Great" or "Great One," reflects her significance in these areas. Tawaret is a composite deity, depicted as a bipedal female figure with the head of a hippopotamus, the limbs and paws of a lion, the back and tail of a crocodile, and the breasts of a human woman. This amalgamation of features from different animals associated with danger and power symbolized her role as a fierce protector.

The hippopotamus aspect of Tawaret was particularly significant, as female hippos are known for their strong maternal instincts and aggressive protection of their young. This made Tawaret a fitting deity to oversee and protect the process of childbirth, a time viewed as fraught with peril in ancient Egypt. She was also seen as a nurturing goddess due to her association with the Nile River, which was vital for life in Egypt.

Tawaret was not part of the official state religion or worshipped in large temples; instead, her worship was more personal and domestic. Pregnant women, in particular, would invoke her protection using amulets, small household shrines, and other magical objects. Her image was often used in household items, such as headrests and pottery, to invoke her protective qualities.

Additionally, Tawaret was sometimes associated with the god Bes, another protective deity, and the two were believed to work together to protect households, particularly during childbirth and in caring for young children. Her role extends beyond just a goddess of childbirth; she was a general protector against evil forces, reflecting the ancient Egyptians' emphasis on the protective powers of the deities in their everyday lives.

Bes

Bes is a distinctive and unique deity in Egyptian mythology, known for his role as a protector of households, particularly of mothers, children, and childbirth. Unlike many Egyptian gods who are often depicted in a somewhat idealized human form, Bes is portrayed quite differently. He is shown as a dwarf, often bearded, with lion-like features, wide eyes, a protruding tongue, and sometimes with the ears and tail of a lion. His appearance, which might seem fearsome or comical, was actually intended to scare off evil spirits and bad luck.

Bes's origins are somewhat mysterious and are thought to be foreign, possibly from Africa or the Middle East. He became popular in Egypt from the Middle Kingdom onwards and was embraced into the Egyptian pantheon as a protector. His image was often used in amulets, on furniture, and in household items, reflecting his role as a guardian deity. He was particularly associated with music, dance, and merrymaking, which were believed to drive away evil spirits. Thus, he was also a god of entertainment, often depicted playing musical instruments like the tambourine.

In addition to his protective role, Bes was also a deity of fertility and sexuality, and was invoked during childbirth to protect the mother and the newborn child. He was believed to be a defender against all that is bad, including snakes, scorpions, and various evil spirits, which made him a popular figure in everyday Egyptian life.

Heqet

Heqet, in Egyptian mythology, is an ancient goddess primarily associated with fertility, childbirth, and rebirth. She is depicted as a frog, or more commonly, as a woman with the head of a frog. This association with frogs likely stems from the Egyptians observing the abundance of frogs around the Nile, especially during the annual inundation, which was a time of fertility and growth for the land.

The frog was seen as a symbol of life and fertility due to its prolific nature and its role in the ecosystem of the Nile. Heqet's image was used in amulets and other objects as a symbol of fertility and protection, particularly for women in childbirth. She was believed to have powers to hasten and ease the process of birth, and it was common for midwives and pregnant women to wear amulets depicting Heqet for protection and aid during labor

In addition to her association with fertility and childbirth, Heqet's role also extended into the realm of the afterlife and resurrection. This is partly due to the frog's life cycle - from tadpole to frog - which was seen as a metaphor for rebirth and transformation. In the funerary context, Heqet was believed to assist in the rebirth of the deceased in the afterlife, paralleling her role in assisting the birth of children in the mortal world.

Khonsu

Khonsu, in Egyptian mythology, is a god associated with the moon, time, and healing. His name means "Traveler," which reflects his role as a lunar deity, moving across the night sky. Khonsu was often depicted as a young man with a side lock of youth, wearing a lunar disk and crescent on his head. He could also be shown as a child or as a falcon-headed man, highlighting his connection to other deities like Horus.

Khonsu's role in the Egyptian pantheon evolved over time. In earlier periods, he was primarily seen as a god of the moon. The moon's phases and its power to illuminate the night made it an important celestial body in ancient Egyptian religion. The changing phases of the moon were also associated with the cycles of time and thus with Khonsu. His lunar aspect linked him with fertility, regeneration, and the passage of time.

As a healing god, Khonsu was believed to have significant power. It was thought that he could drive out evil spirits and was often invoked in healing rituals and spells. His abilities as a healer were sometimes merged with other deities like Thoth, another god of the moon and wisdom.

Khonsu was part of a Theban triad of deities, along with Amun, the king of the gods, and Mut, the mother goddess. In this triad, Khonsu is often considered the son of Amun and Mut. The cult of Khonsu gained prominence during the New Kingdom, particularly at Thebes, where he was worshipped at the Karnak Temple complex along with his parents.

Seshat

Seshat, in Egyptian mythology, is a goddess who is often overlooked but plays a significant and unique role as the deity of writing, wisdom, and knowledge. She is depicted as a woman wearing a panther-skin dress (a garment associated with funerary priests) and a headdress that is typically a seven-pointed emblem or a star with a bow on top. Sometimes she is also shown with a palm stem, used by the ancient Egyptians to denote years, thereby associating her with the recording of time.

Seshat's primary role was as the goddess of writing and scribes. She was seen as the divine record-keeper and was often depicted inscribing the names and titles of pharaohs on the leaves of the tree of life, ensuring their immortality. She was also involved in recording the spoils and captives taken in battle, as well as keeping records of the foundation and dimensions of temples and other important structures. This made her an important deity in the context of the construction and maintenance of monuments and in the administration of the kingdom.

In addition to her role in writing and record-keeping, Seshat was also associated with wisdom, knowledge, and architecture. She was often thought of as the female counterpart or consort to Thoth, the god of wisdom, writing, and magic. Together, they were believed to be the source of all knowledge in the world, encompassing both the sacred and the mundane.

Wadjet

Wadjet, in Egyptian mythology, is an ancient and powerful goddess, known as one of the earliest deities of the Egyptian pantheon. She is often depicted as a cobra or as a woman with the head of a cobra, symbolizing her role as a protector and a fierce guardian. Wadjet was also associated with royalty, and her image was frequently used as a symbol of the Pharaoh's power and divine authority.

Wadjet's origins can be traced back to the pre-dynastic period in Egypt, and she was primarily worshipped in the city of Buto (Per-Wadjet) in the Nile Delta. As the patron goddess of Lower Egypt, she was one of the two protective deities for ancient Egypt, the other being Nekhbet, the vulture goddess, who was the patron of Upper Egypt. Together, they were known as the "Two Ladies," representing the unification of the two regions of Egypt under a single Pharaoh.

One of Wadjet's most significant roles was as the protector of the Pharaoh and the Egyptian lands. Her image was often used in the "uraeus," the rearing cobra symbol adorning the crowns of the Pharaohs, symbolizing her protective powers. The uraeus was believed to spit fire at the enemies of the Pharaoh, offering him divine protection. As a goddess of sovereignty, she was also associated with the Eye of Ra, a powerful symbol of the sun god's wrath and power.

Wadjet's worship continued throughout the history of ancient Egypt, reflecting her enduring significance as a goddess of protection, royalty, and fertility. Her image and symbols remained powerful state emblems, and her cult was one of the most enduring in the Egyptian religious landscape, highlighting her integral role in the spiritual and political life of ancient Egypt.

Chapter 2: Other Characters

In addition to the many Gods and Goddesses discussed in Chapter 1, the ancient Egyptian myths are host to several different characters and creatures. In this chapter, we'll introduce you to some of the characters you'll encounter in Egyptian mythology.

Imhotep

Imhotep, in Egyptian mythology and history, is a figure who blurs the lines between myth and reality. Historically, Imhotep was a high-ranking advisor, priest, architect, and physician who lived during the Third Dynasty of Egypt, serving under the Pharaoh Djoser. He is most famously credited with designing the Step Pyramid at Saqqara, one of the earliest known pyramids, around 2600 BC. This accomplishment made him renowned as one of the world's first named architects.

In mythology and later Egyptian culture, Imhotep's reputation grew to almost divine status. Over centuries, his historical persona merged with that of a god. He was venerated as a god of medicine and healing, and temples were dedicated to him where people would seek cures for their ailments. By the Late Period of ancient Egyptian history, he was fully deified, worshipped as a son of Ptah, the god of craftsmen and architects, in Memphis. His cult following continued well into the Ptolemaic and Roman periods in Egypt.

Imhotep's unique status as a historical figure who transcended into the realm of gods is rare in Egyptian mythology. He is an example of how, in ancient cultures, the lines between history and myth could become blurred, elevating a mortal to a position of divine reverence due to his significant contributions and lasting legacy.

Pharaohs

In Egyptian mythology and society, Pharaohs occupied a central and complex role, serving not only as rulers but also as intermediaries between the gods and the people. The Pharaoh was considered a divine or semi-divine figure, often thought to be the physical embodiment or son of a god, typically Ra, the sun god. This divinity bestowed upon the Pharaoh a unique position in both the religious and political spheres of ancient Egyptian life.

The role of the Pharaoh was multifaceted. As a political leader, the Pharaoh was the supreme ruler of Egypt, possessing absolute power over the land and its people. This included responsibilities for making laws, waging war, and governing the people. The Pharaoh was also seen as a protector of the realm, responsible for maintaining Ma'at – the ancient Egyptian concept of truth, balance, order, law, morality, and justice.

In a religious context, the Pharaoh's duties were equally significant. He was responsible for maintaining the gods' favor, a role that involved building great temples, making offerings, and conducting rituals. The prosperity and well-being of the country were believed to directly depend on the Pharaoh's ability to appease the gods and uphold Ma'at. After death, the Pharaoh was thought to ascend to the afterlife, where he would continue to play a role in maintaining the cosmic order.

The Bennu

The Bennu in Egyptian mythology is a mythological bird that holds a significant place in the ancient Egyptian belief system. Often associated with the sun, creation, and rebirth, the Bennu is akin to the Phoenix in Greek mythology. The name 'Bennu' itself is thought to be derived from the word 'weben,' meaning 'to rise' or 'to shine,' a reference to its connections with the sun.

The Bennu bird is often depicted as a large, grey heron with a long beak and a two-feathered crest, sometimes with a solar disk crowning its head, emphasizing its relationship with the sun god Ra. According to myth, the Bennu bird played a role in the creation of the world. It was believed to have arisen from the waters of chaos at the beginning of time, bringing existence into being. This act of emergence and creation linked the Bennu with aspects of rebirth and renewal.

The Bennu was also connected to the Egyptian solar cycle and the concept of rebirth in the afterlife. It was believed that the bird lived for hundreds of years before it burned itself to death and then rose anew from its own ashes, symbolizing the cycle of death and rebirth. This made the Bennu a symbol of resurrection and eternal life, and it was often associated with Osiris, the god of the afterlife, and resurrection in Egyptian mythology.

Apep (Apophis)

Apep, also known as Apophis in Greek, is a malevolent figure in ancient Egyptian mythology, embodying chaos, darkness, and evil. He is often depicted as a giant serpent or snake, representing the antithesis of Ma'at, the concept of truth, order, and harmony that was central to Egyptian belief.

Apep's primary role in Egyptian mythology is as the eternal enemy of Ra, the sun god. Each night, as Ra travels through the underworld in his solar boat, Apep attempts to devour him, an act that would bring about the end of the world by plunging it into eternal darkness and chaos. This struggle represents the constant battle between order (Ma'at) and chaos (Isfet). The defeat of Apep by Ra, or sometimes by Ra's protectors, such as the god Set, ensures the sunrise and the continuation of life. This daily victory over Apep was considered essential for the maintenance of the cosmos and the order of the world.

Apep was not worshipped; instead, he was feared and reviled. Ancient Egyptians performed daily rituals to help Ra and to ward off Apep, often involving spells and incantations. There were also more physical manifestations of these rituals, such as the creation of amulets and the holding of ceremonial practices intended to protect the sun god and ensure his rebirth every morning.

The Sphinx

The Sphinx in Egyptian mythology is a mythical creature with the body of a lion and the head of a human, often associated with wisdom, strength, and mystery. The most famous representation of a Sphinx is the Great Sphinx of Giza, which is one of the most iconic symbols of ancient Egypt. While the Sphinx appears in various forms and myths in different cultures, in Egyptian context, it holds a special place, often associated with guardianship and protection.

In Egyptian mythology, the Sphinx is not a specific deity but rather a symbolic representation. The lion's body symbolizes royal power, strength, and authority, while the human head is thought to represent intelligence and wisdom. The combination of these features makes the Sphinx a potent symbol of the

Pharaoh's power and wisdom, embodying both the physical strength of a lion and the intellectual and ruling power of the king.

The Sphinxes were often placed at the entrances of temples and pyramids as guardians. They were believed to ward off evil spirits and protect the sacred spaces within. The Great Sphinx of Giza, which lies near the Great Pyramids, is thought to be a guardian of the Giza plateau and is often associated with the Pharaoh Khafre, whose pyramid complex is nearby.

The Sebau

The Sebau (or Seba) in Egyptian mythology refer to a group of malevolent beings or demons. They are less well-known than many of the major gods and goddesses but play a significant role in the Egyptian cosmological and mythological framework, particularly in relation to themes of chaos and disorder.

The Sebau were often depicted as humanoid figures with animalistic features, such as the heads of dangerous animals like crocodiles or with other fearsome attributes. Their portrayal was intended to evoke fear and revulsion, symbolizing their role as agents of chaos and destruction. They were often seen as opponents of the cosmic order, or Ma'at, which was the principle of truth, balance, and harmony that was central to Egyptian religion and society.

In Egyptian mythology, the Sebau were frequently portrayed as adversaries of the sun god Ra. Each night, as Ra journeyed through the underworld in his solar barque, he had to confront and overcome various obstacles, including the Sebau. These demons represented the forces of chaos and darkness that sought to prevent the sun's rebirth and the continuation of the cosmic order. The defeat of the Sebau each night was crucial for the maintenance of balance in the universe and the assurance of Ra's reemergence in the morning.

The Sebau were not worshipped; rather, they were feared and reviled as embodiments of all that was antithetical to the ordered and structured world the Egyptians strived to maintain.

Chapter 3: Egyptian Creation Myths

Unlike many other mythologies, Egyptian mythology doesn't have just one creation myth. Rather, there have been many different creation myths emerge throughout the long history of ancient Egypt, each from different areas of the country.

There are four prominent creation myths in Egyptian mythology, which we will cover in this chapter. They are the Heliopolitan Creation Myth (from Heliopolis), the Memphite Creation Myth (from Memphis), the Hermopolitan Creation Myth (from Hermopolis), and the Theban Creation Myth (from Thebes).

Heliopolitan Creation Myth

The Heliopolitan Creation Myth is one of the most significant and influential creation stories in ancient Egyptian mythology, originating from Heliopolis, an ancient city near present-day Cairo. This myth centers around the god Atum and the creation of the world and the gods.

In the beginning, there was only the primordial waters of chaos, known as Nun. From these chaotic waters, a mound of earth emerged, and upon it stood Atum, the first god, who was self-created or born out of these waters. Atum is often depicted as a serpent or in human form. As a solitary being, he embodied the potential for all creation but was initially alone in the void.

Seeking to create others, Atum began the process of creation through a combination of self-pleasure and spitting or sneezing. From this act, he produced Shu, the god of air, and Tefnut, the goddess of moisture or mist. Shu and Tefnut went on to give birth to two children, Geb, the god of the earth, and Nut, the goddess of the sky. This divine family represented the primary elements of the world - air, moisture, earth, and sky.

Geb and Nut's union was initially so close that there was no space between them, meaning there was no place where life could exist. Shu intervened to separate them, lifting Nut high above Geb, creating the space in which the mortal world exists. Nut and Geb became the parents of Osiris, Isis, Seth, and Nephthys, who were central figures in Egyptian mythology.

The myth also describes the cyclical journey of the sun god, Ra (or Re), who is closely associated with Atum. Ra travels across the sky in his solar boat, representing the passage of the day. At night, he travels through the underworld, where he defeats the forces of chaos to be reborn each morning.

In the Heliopolitan cosmogony, the act of creation is ongoing. Pharaohs, viewed as divine rulers, were often associated with Atum, and their reigns were seen as a continuation of the creative process. The myth provided a framework for understanding the order of the universe, the roles of the gods, and the place of humans within this order.

Memphite Creation Myth

The Memphite Creation Myth is an ancient Egyptian narrative of the creation of the world, originating from Memphis, one of the oldest and most important cities in ancient Egypt. This myth places Ptah, the god of craftsmen and architects, at the center of creation, offering a unique perspective compared to the Heliopolitan Creation Myth which focuses on Atum.

According to the Memphite Creation Myth, Ptah existed in the primordial waters of chaos before the beginning of time. Unlike the Heliopolitan myth, which involves a physical generation of gods through procreation, the Memphite myth emphasizes the power of the word and the mind. Ptah is said to have created the world through thought and speech. He conceived the world in his heart (mind) and then brought it into existence by his command, which is the spoken word.

This idea aligns with the role of Ptah as the patron god of artisans, sculptors, and builders. Just as a craftsman first conceives an idea in his mind and then realizes it in physical form, Ptah first envisioned creation in his mind and then spoke it into existence. This emphasis on thought and speech highlights the power of intellect and creativity, reflecting the high regard ancient Egyptians had for these attributes.

The Memphite Creation Myth also includes other deities as manifestations of Ptah's creative will. It is said that Atum and the other gods were created through Ptah's heart and tongue. Thus, Ptah is seen not only as a primary creator god but also as the source of the power of other gods. The myth suggests that all of creation, including the gods and the physical world, is the result of Ptah's creative thought and word.

Another important aspect of the Memphite myth is the concept of Ma'at, the principle of truth, balance, and cosmic order. Ptah is seen as the one who established Ma'at, ensuring that the universe operates according to a harmonious and balanced order. This established the king's role in maintaining Ma'at in the earthly realm, as the representative of Ptah.

Hermopolitan Creation Myth

The Hermopolitan Creation Myth is one of the ancient Egyptian cosmogonies, originating from the city of Hermopolis, also known as Khmunu. This myth is distinct from the Heliopolitan and Memphite creation myths, as it focuses on the Ogdoad, a group of eight primordial deities, and emphasizes the role of the god Thoth.

In the Hermopolitan myth, the universe began as a vast, inert body of water, the primordial ocean called Nun. Within this chaotic, undifferentiated expanse, the Ogdoad existed. The Ogdoad was comprised of four pairs of male and female deities, each representing fundamental aspects of the primeval world. They were Nun and Naunet (representing the primordial water), Heh and Hauhet (infinity or eternity), Kek and Kauket (darkness), and Amun and Amaunet (hiddenness or obscurity).

These deities were thought to exist in the darkness and chaos of Nun, symbolizing the potential for life and creation. They were associated with different elements of the primordial world and played a crucial role in the process of creation. The Ogdoad deities were not creators themselves but rather the elements from which creation eventually emerged.

According to the myth, the interaction and intermingling of these primordial forces eventually led to the emergence of a primeval mound, symbolizing the first emergence of solid land from the waters of chaos. Upon this mound, the first god, often identified as Ra or Atum in different versions of the myth, came into being. This deity then proceeded with the act of creation, bringing forth the other gods, humans, and the world as we know it.

An essential aspect of the Hermopolitan myth is the emphasis on the power of speech in the creation process. The god Thoth, who was the deity of wisdom, knowledge, and writing, and who later became closely associated with Hermopolis, played a significant role in this regard. Thoth was believed to have used his powers of divine speech to give form and order to the creation initiated by the first god.

The Hermopolitan Creation Myth is notable for its abstract and somewhat philosophical nature, focusing on the emergence of life from non-life and the transformation of chaos into order. It highlights the complexity of ancient Egyptian religious thought, where different centers of worship developed their own interpretations of the creation of the world, each emphasizing different aspects of the divine and the cosmos.

Theban Creation Myth

The Theban Creation Myth, originating from the city of Thebes in ancient Egypt, represents another unique perspective on the creation of the world within Egyptian mythology. This myth rose to prominence during the Middle and New Kingdom periods when Thebes became a major religious and political center. The central figure in the Theban myth is the god Amun, who later merged with the sun god Ra to become Amun-Ra, a composite deity representing both hidden power and the visible sun.

In the Theban creation narrative, Amun-Ra is considered the primeval creator, a self-generated deity who existed before all things. Unlike other creation myths where creation starts with a physical or tangible element (such as the primordial waters in the Heliopolitan or Hermopolitan myths), the Theban myth emphasizes the mysterious and hidden nature of Amun. As a god who is both invisible and omnipresent, Amun-Ra's creation act is seen as a divine mystery, something beyond human understanding.

According to the myth, Amun-Ra, in his aspect of the hidden god, created himself out of nothing, emerging spontaneously. He then created all the gods and everything in the universe by the power of his thought and word. In some versions of the myth, it is said that he first created Ptah, the god of craftsmen, who then helped realize the creation envisioned by Amun-Ra.

Amun-Ra's role as a creator god is also tied to his aspect as the sun god, Ra. The sun's journey across the sky and through the underworld was seen as a daily process of death and rebirth, a cycle that mirrored the creation of the world. The sun was a symbol of life-giving energy and renewal, and Amun-Ra's identity as the sun god reinforced his role as the source of all life.

The Theban myth also places great emphasis on Ma'at, the concept of cosmic order and balance. Amun-Ra was seen as the upholder of Ma'at, and by extension, the Pharaoh, as the representative of Amun-Ra on earth, was responsible for maintaining this order.

The Theban Creation Myth reflects the political and religious ascendancy of Thebes, especially during the New Kingdom when the worship of Amun-Ra became state-sponsored. This myth differs from others in its focus on a single, hidden, and mysterious creator deity, showcasing the diversity and complexity of Egyptian religious beliefs and their capacity to evolve and adapt to the changing political and social landscape of ancient Egypt.

Chapter 4: Osiris and Set

Osiris was a king of Egypt, revered not only for his just rule but also for bringing agriculture and civilization to his people. Under his guidance, Egypt knew peace and prosperity, and the land was fruitful. Osiris was married to his sister, Isis, a wise and magical goddess who was loved throughout the land. Together, they presided over a golden age in Egypt.

But in the shadows lurked Osiris's brother, Set, a being of violence and envy. Unlike his brother, Set was associated with the harsh desert, storms, and disorder. Set resented Osiris's popularity and power, and he plotted to usurp his throne.

Set's plan was cunning. He hosted a lavish banquet, inviting gods and important figures from across Egypt. Among the evening's entertainments was a beautifully crafted chest, inlaid with precious metals and stones. Set declared that he would give this chest to whomever it fit perfectly. One by one, guests lay in the chest, but none fit until Osiris stepped in. As soon as Osiris lay down, Set slammed the chest shut, sealing it with lead, and threw it into the Nile.

The chest floated down the Nile and out to sea, eventually coming to rest in a great tamarisk tree growing near Byblos. The tree, embracing the divine essence of Osiris, grew rapidly, encasing the chest within its trunk. The king of Byblos, marveling at the tree's size and fragrance, ordered it cut down to be made into a pillar for his palace, not knowing the chest and Osiris lay within.

Back in Egypt, Isis was frantic. She cut her hair in mourning and set out to find her husband. Her search was long and full of hardships, but she was relentless. Her search was guided by her deep love and magical intuition. Upon arriving in Byblos, she found the tree containing Osiris's body but had to devise a way to retrieve it. Isis, known for her wisdom and magical prowess, cunningly ingratiated herself with the royal court. She became the nursemaid to the royal child, using her divine powers to protect and nurture the infant.

In one version of the myth, she revealed her divine nature to the queen and, in gratitude for her services, was granted the pillar — the tamarisk tree containing Osiris's body. In another version, she revealed her goddess nature to the king and queen and explained her quest to retrieve her husband's body. Moved by her story and her divine status, the king agreed to give her the pillar.

Isis then retrieved Osiris's body from the tree and returned to Egypt, where she hid it in the marshes of the Nile Delta while she set out to gather herbs to perform the rites to resurrect Osiris.

However, Set, ever vigilant and intent on thwarting his brother's return to life, was out hunting by the Nile one night. The exact details of how he came upon the chest vary in different versions of the myth. In some accounts, it is by chance — Set, while hunting, happens to come across the secluded spot where Isis hid the chest. In others, it's implied that Set was actively searching for Osiris's body, guided by suspicion or informants who had seen Isis or the chest.

In some versions of the story, it is said that Set's attention was drawn to the chest when his hunting dogs caught the scent of Osiris's body or when the moonlight reflected off the chest, revealing its location among the reeds. In others, Set's discovery of the chest is more of an intentional search, with Set scouring the land, driven by his hatred and jealousy towards Osiris.

Regardless of the method, Set's discovery of Osiris's body is a pivotal moment in the story. Set, upon discovering the chest, tore Osiris's body into fourteen pieces, scattering them across Egypt.

Isis, often accompanied by her sister Nephthys, traveled throughout Egypt in search of the pieces of Osiris's body. Each time she found a piece, she performed rituals to honor it and preserve it. With the help of other deities like Anubis, the god of embalming, and Thoth, the god of wisdom and magic, she was able to reassemble Osiris's body, except for one crucial part.

The missing piece was Osiris's phallus, which was said to have been thrown into the Nile and eaten by a fish (often described as an oxyrhynchus fish) or, in some versions, by a crocodile. This loss symbolized Osiris's death and his role in the underworld, as he could no longer be a living, procreative being.

Isis, undeterred by the missing piece, used her magical powers to fashion a replacement for the missing part, thereby completing Osiris's body. Through her spells and rituals, she temporarily resurrected Osiris, long enough to conceive their son, Horus.

After being resurrected by Isis through her magic, could not remain in the realm of the living for long. He became the ruler of the underworld, known as the Duat. This transition marked a significant shift in his role within the pantheon of Egyptian gods.

As the lord of the underworld, Osiris presided over the judgment of the dead. In this capacity, he became the judge who weighed the hearts of the deceased against the feather of Ma'at, the concept of truth and cosmic order. This ritual determined whether a soul was worthy of entering the afterlife. Osiris, therefore, became a symbol of resurrection and eternal life.

Chapter 5: The Contendings of Horus and Set

In the pantheon of ancient Egyptian mythology, the Contendings of Horus and Set stands as one of the most intricate and enduring stories. This mythological narrative, rich in symbolism and allegory, explores themes of rightful rulership, the balance of power, and the eternal struggle between order and chaos. It unfolds in a series of trials, challenges, and divine judgments, showcasing the complexity of ancient Egyptian beliefs.

After Osiris was cunningly murdered and dismembered by Set, his consort Isis, through her magic and determination, managed to resurrect him long enough to conceive their son, Horus. Raised in secret and nurtured by his mother's wisdom and magic, Horus grew to embody the rightful claim to the throne of Egypt, a claim that Set vehemently disputed.

The gods, aware of the brewing conflict, convened a great tribunal to resolve the matter. Led by Ra, the sun god, this divine council witnessed the adamant claims of both Horus and Set. Ra, initially swayed by Set's strength and assertive nature, seemed inclined towards the god of chaos, but Isis and others argued fervently for Horus's right to rule.

In order to determine who the rightful ruler should be, the council suggested that Set and Horus compete in a series of challenges. The contests were varied, ranging from physical battles to cunning tests, each revealing different aspects of the contenders' strengths and weaknesses.

In the first test, both Horus and Set were tasked with constructing a boat and racing it on the Nile. The winner of the race would be considered stronger and more deserving of the throne.

Set, known for his strength and formidable power, opted to build his boat out of heavy timber. He constructed a sturdy and imposing vessel, confident in its ability to navigate the Nile and secure his victory. Set's choice reflected his nature – direct, forceful, and reliant on physical prowess.

Horus, on the other hand, employed a more cunning approach. Understanding that he could not outmatch Set in a contest of pure strength, Horus built his boat out of papyrus, a light and buoyant material commonly found along the banks of the Nile. Papyrus boats were a familiar sight in ancient Egypt, known for their agility and speed. However, to deceive Set and the council of gods, Horus ingeniously crafted his papyrus boat to resemble a stone vessel. This disguise was intended to give the impression of a heavy, cumbersome boat, misleading Set into underestimating Horus's chances in the race.

On the day of the race, both gods launched their boats into the Nile. Set's heavy wooden boat, despite its robust appearance, was ill-suited to the race. Its weight and cumbersome build proved to be a disadvantage. Meanwhile, Horus's disguised papyrus boat was light and nimble, easily gliding over the waters of the Nile.

As the race commenced, the outcome became quickly apparent. Set's boat, unable to sustain its bulk, sank into the Nile almost immediately after setting off. Horus, meanwhile, skillfully navigated his seemingly stone but actually light and agile papyrus boat, swiftly moving along the river.

In another contest, Horus and Set agreed to transform themselves into hippopotamuses and submerge themselves in the Nile River. The terms of the challenge were that they had to remain underwater for three months, demonstrating their strength and endurance. The hippopotamus was chosen as it was a creature known for its immense power and aggression, symbolizing the formidable nature of both Horus and Set.

As the challenge commenced, both gods transformed into hippopotamuses and plunged into the Nile. Their enormous forms submerged, and they settled beneath the waters, beginning their long wait. This act of submerging was symbolic, representing not only physical strength but also the ability to endure and maintain power under difficult conditions.

Isis, ever protective of her son Horus, watched the contest with growing concern. As the days passed, she became increasingly worried that Horus would not be able to outlast Set. Determined to ensure her son's victory, Isis decided to intervene, despite the rules of the challenge.

Crafting a harpoon, Isis targeted Set while he was submerged. However, when she struck Set, he called out to her, appealing to her as his sister. Isis, struck by a moment of compassion, relented and helped Set. This act of mercy, however, infuriated Horus. Feeling betrayed by his mother's interference, Horus emerged from the water in a rage. In some versions of the myth, Horus even decapitates Isis, though she is later healed by Thoth.

The gods witnessing the event were taken aback by the turn of events. The challenge, meant to be a fair test of strength and endurance, had turned into a chaotic display of familial strife and emotional upheaval where there was no clear victor.

In the context of their ongoing struggle, Set devised a plan to undermine Horus's claim to the throne by attempting to dominate him sexually. Set believed that by doing so, he could demonstrate Horus's weakness and his own superiority, thereby legitimizing his claim to rule Egypt. According to the myth, Set attempted to secretly ejaculate on Horus, with the intention of later declaring to the council of gods that Horus was his submissive.

However, Horus, forewarned by his mother, Isis, caught Set's semen in his hand. Horus then went to his mother, who devised a counterplan. Isis took Horus's semen and secretly applied it to some lettuce, a food that Set regularly consumed. Set, unknowingly ate the lettuce, thus ingested Horus's semen.

When the time came for the council of gods to convene and pass judgment, Set proudly proclaimed his dominance over Horus, believing his plot had succeeded. However, to determine the truth, the gods called forth the semen of Horus, and it responded by emerging as a golden sun disk from Set's forehead. Alternatively, in some versions, it called forth the semen of Set, but it did not respond from Horus, proving Set's claim false. In a strange turn of events, Set's plan had backfired, but the council of Gods were still undecided over who the ruler of Egypt should be.

In the next challenge, Horus and Set were tasked to prove their strength and divine power by moving heavy stones. The challenge was likely designed to test not just their physical might but also their ability to wield divine, supernatural strength.

Set, confident in his immense physical power as the god of storms and chaos, saw this as an opportunity to assert his dominance. He was known for his brute strength and was considered one of the most powerful gods in terms of physical prowess.

As the challenge commenced, both Horus and Set attempted to move enormous stones, possibly using their divine powers. In some versions of the myth, the challenge involved not just moving the stones but also hurling them or placing them at great distances to demonstrate their strength and control over the forces of nature.

However, the outcome of this challenge, like many others in the contendings, is not well-documented in ancient sources, and different versions of the myth offer varying accounts. In some, Horus outmaneuvers Set, using clever tactics or magical intervention, much as he did in the boat race. In others, the challenge ends inconclusively, further prolonging the dispute over the throne of Egypt.

Following the various contests, which showcased both the strengths and weaknesses of Horus and Set, the gods assembled once again to deliver their final judgment. The prolonged conflict and the series of inconclusive challenges had left the gods divided.

In some versions of the myth, it is the wisdom of the goddess Neith, known for her intelligence and fairness, that sways the council. She suggests that Horus is the rightful ruler of Egypt, as he is the legitimate heir of Osiris. Neith also proposes compensating Set to appease him and prevent further discord. Her suggestions are well-received by the council.

In other versions, the god Thoth, known for his role as the arbitrator and keeper of divine order, plays a crucial role in the final judgment. Thoth's wisdom and knowledge of Ma'at (cosmic order and truth) are instrumental in reaching a decision that upholds the principles of justice and rightful succession.

Ultimately, the gods decree that Horus, the son of Osiris and Isis, is the rightful ruler of Egypt. Horus's ascent to the throne symbolizes the restoration of order and the continuation of the dynastic lineage. He is seen as the embodiment of the rightful pharaoh, upholding Ma'at and ruling with justice.

Set, on the other hand, is not destroyed or banished, which is significant. In a gesture that underscores the importance of reconciliation and balance, Set is given a new role. He is often depicted as accompanying Ra, the sun god, on his nightly journey through the underworld, defending the solar barque from the serpent Apophis, embodying chaos and destruction. This role for Set acknowledges his strength and power, channeling them towards the protection of the cosmic order rather than its disruption.

Chapter 6: Ra's Journey Through the Underworld

The story of Ra's nightly journey through the underworld is a tale of mystery, danger, and the eternal cycle of life, death, and rebirth. Each night, as the sun god Ra set in the west, he embarked on a perilous journey through the Duat, the Egyptian underworld, only to be reborn at dawn, bringing light back to the world.

As the sun disappeared from the sky, Ra, in the form of a ram-headed deity, boarded his magnificent solar barque, the Mesektet boat, to begin his nocturnal voyage. This journey was not merely a passage of time but a crucial event in maintaining the balance of the cosmos. The underworld was a place of great danger, inhabited by serpents, monsters, and demons, all personifications of chaos and destruction.

Ra's barque was not alone on this journey. He was accompanied by a retinue of gods and goddesses, each playing a vital role in safeguarding the sun god and ensuring the continuation of the cycle. Among them were Set, the god of chaos, who protected the solar barque from the greatest threat in the underworld, the monstrous serpent Apep (or Apophis). Apep represented the ultimate force of chaos and destruction, and each night it sought to stop Ra, engulfing the world into eternal darkness.

The battle with Apep was a central moment of the journey. Set, standing at the prow of the barque, would bravely fend off the serpent with his spear, while other deities used their magic to weaken and repel it. This fight was not a mere physical struggle but a battle of cosmic significance, symbolizing the ongoing struggle between order and chaos, light and darkness.

As the barque journeyed through the twelve hours of the night, corresponding to the twelve sections of the underworld, Ra passed through various gates, each guarded by fearsome gatekeepers and requiring secret passwords to pass. These gates represented different stages of the night and the dangers that lurked within them. Ra had to use all his wisdom and power to navigate these obstacles.

In addition to battling external threats, Ra's journey was also a process of rejuvenation and regeneration. He merged with Osiris, the god of the dead and ruler of the underworld, symbolizing the unity of life and death, the interconnection of the sun and the earth. This union was essential for Ra's rebirth at dawn, as it imbued him with the life-giving aspects of Osiris, ensuring the continuity of life and the cyclical nature of time.

As dawn approached, Ra emerged victorious from the underworld, reborn and revitalized. His barque, now the Mandjet boat, appeared in the eastern horizon, bringing light, warmth, and life back to the world. The daily triumph of Ra over the forces of chaos and darkness was a cause for celebration and relief, reaffirming the stability and order of the cosmos.

This myth, more than a mere story, was a fundamental expression of the ancient Egyptian understanding of the universe. The nightly journey of Ra through the underworld encapsulated their beliefs about death and rebirth, the eternal struggle between order and chaos, and the cyclical nature of time and existence.

Chapter 7: The Tale of Two Brothers

"The Tale of Two Brothers" is a story rich with intrigue, betrayal, and magic, blending the themes of familial loyalty and the complexities of fate. This tale, handed down through generations, speaks of two brothers, Anubis and Bata, whose lives were intertwined with both divine favor and grave misfortune.

Anubis, the elder brother, was a prosperous farmer, happily married, and lived a life of contentment. His younger brother, Bata, was strong and handsome, with a remarkable ability to understand animals. They shared a deep bond, with Bata working the fields alongside Anubis and living under his roof.

One day, as fate would have it, Anubis's wife, struck by Bata's youthful charm and strength, attempted to seduce him. Bata, horrified by her advances, rebuffed her, swearing to tell no one of the incident. However, the scorned wife, fearing reprisal, crafted a deceitful plan. She feigned illness and, when questioned by Anubis, accused Bata of assaulting her.

Enraged and feeling betrayed, Anubis set out to kill his brother. Bata, warned by the cattle he could understand, fled. As Anubis pursued him, the gods intervened, creating a great river filled with crocodiles to separate the brothers and allow Bata to explain his innocence. Bata, in an attempt to prove his innocence, cut off his penis and threw it into the river, where it was swallowed by a fish. Convinced of his brother's integrity, Anubis returned home, ashamed and regretful.

Bata then headed to the Valley of the Pine, where the gods, impressed by his righteousness, helped him create a wife from his rib to keep him company. This wife was of such extraordinary beauty that her fame spread across the land, eventually reaching the ears of the Pharaoh. Intrigued by the tales of her beauty, the Pharaoh decided to see her for himself.

In some versions of the story, Bata's wife left him willingly, attracted by the prospect of becoming the queen and leaving her modest life behind. In other versions, she was taken against her will by the Pharaoh's men, but once in the palace, she adapted to her new life and status, abandoning her loyalty to Bata.

Meanwhile, Bata, heartbroken, transformed himself into a bull and returned to his brother. Transforming himself into a bull was a mystical display of Bata's connection with the divine powers, a last resort to reunite with his brother Anubis.

Upon his return, Bata, now in the form of a magnificent bull, went to the fields where his brother Anubis was working. Anubis, upon seeing the bull, felt an inexplicable connection to the creature. Despite not knowing the bull's true identity, Anubis felt drawn to it and decided to take it home. The bull was treated with great care and affection, becoming a beloved part of Anubis's household.

However, the story took a tragic turn when the Pharaoh heard about this extraordinary bull. Intrigued by the descriptions of its beauty and majesty, the Pharaoh wanted to see the animal for himself. Upon witnessing the bull, the Pharaoh was struck by its magnificence and decided that such a splendid creature should be offered as a sacrifice to the gods, a common practice in ancient Egypt for animals seen as embodying divine qualities.

Anubis, unaware that the bull was, in fact, his brother Bata, was devastated by the thought of losing the animal he had grown so fond of. He reluctantly sent the bull to the Pharaoh, grieving the loss. Bata, understanding his fate, accepted it as a necessary step in the unfolding of their destiny.

During the sacrifice, as the bull was killed, a miracle occurred. From the blood of the bull, two persea trees sprang up beside the altar, a symbolic representation of Bata's enduring spirit and his connection to the divine. These trees, embodying Bata's spirit, stood beside the Pharaoh's temple, commanding attention with their sudden and unexplained emergence.

The queen, Bata's former wife who had initially betrayed him, was intrigued by the beauty and fragrance of these trees. As she came near, the trees spoke to her, revealing that they were in fact Bata, whom she had wronged. The revelation shocked the queen, but it also presented her with an opportunity to rid herself of Bata once and for all.

In an act of treachery, she persuaded the Pharaoh to cut down the persea trees, under the guise of wanting to use the beautiful wood to craft furniture. Oblivious to the trees' true nature, the Pharaoh agreed to her request. As the trees were cut down, a splinter from one of them flew into the queen's mouth. This was no ordinary splinter but a part of Bata's essence, and as it entered her body, she became pregnant.

The queen later gave birth to a son, who was none other than a reborn incarnation of Bata. This child grew at a remarkable pace, displaying wisdom and qualities far beyond his years. His divine lineage and extraordinary abilities soon caught the Pharaoh's attention, who took a great liking to the boy and appointed him as his crown prince.

As the prince grew into a young man, the gods endowed him with knowledge of his true identity and past. Armed with this knowledge, he decided to bring the truth about his mother's betrayal to light. He told the Pharaoh the entire story of his life as Bata, his betrayal by the queen, his transformations, and his final rebirth as the Pharaoh's heir.

The Pharaoh, struck by the truth of the prince's words and the divine will evident in his tale, acted swiftly. He punished the queen for her deceit and treachery. As for Bata, now the crown prince, he was elevated to a position of great honor and power, eventually succeeding the Pharaoh as the ruler of Egypt. His brother, Anubis, was also honored and reunited with Bata in a joyous reconciliation.

Chapter 8: Isis and the Seven Scorpions

The story of Isis and the Seven Scorpions is a tale that intertwines themes of power, protection, and the duality of nature. It is a narrative that speaks to the heart of Egyptian religious beliefs, highlighting the protective and nurturing aspects of Isis, one of the most revered goddesses of the Egyptian pantheon.

The tale begins with Isis, in the period following the murder of her husband Osiris by his brother Set. Fearing for the safety of her son Horus, Isis fled into the marshes of the Nile Delta to hide from Set's wrath and to raise her son in secret. Accompanying her were seven scorpions, each with a unique name and role, serving as her guardians and protectors on the journey.

The scorpions were Tefen and Befen, who led the way; Mestet and Mestetef, who guarded her sides; Petet, Thetet, and Maatet, who followed behind, ensuring no harm came from the rear. They were fierce and loyal, ready to strike down any who threatened Isis or the young Horus.

As they journeyed, Isis, cloaked in her magical powers, sought refuge each night, always vigilant of the dangers that lurked. One evening, they approached a town, seeking shelter. Isis, in her disguise as a humble woman, approached a home and asked for refuge. But the woman of the house, recognizing the danger posed by the scorpions, refused her entry.

Rejected, Isis and her companions found shelter in the home of a poor woman, who welcomed them with kindness. While Isis and Horus slept, the scorpions plotted revenge against the woman who had turned them away. They combined their venom into Tefen's sting, and Tefen slipped away to the house of the Two Sisters, where he stung the woman's young son, leaving him near death.

Upon learning of the child's plight, Isis, moved by compassion, decided to help. She demonstrated her dual role as a protector and healer, using her immense magical powers to cure the child. She chanted powerful spells and called upon her knowledge of the secret names of Ra, commanding the poison to retreat. The child was saved, and the townspeople, amazed by the miracle, praised Isis.

This act of healing served a dual purpose. It was a demonstration of Isis's power and a lesson in humility and compassion. For the woman who had turned her away, it was a harsh lesson in the consequences of turning away those in need. For the townspeople, it was a revelation of the divine power that walked among them, disguised yet ever-present.

Chapter 9: Sekhmet and the Destruction of Mankind

In the ancient Egyptian pantheon, few deities were as feared and revered as Sekhmet, the lioness goddess, a being of war and destruction, but also of healing. Her story is a testament to the duality of her nature and the Egyptian understanding of balance and cosmic order.

The tale begins with Ra, the sun god, the ruler of the gods and humanity. In his old age, Ra felt that his authority was being mocked and ignored by humans. Displeased and angry, he called upon the council of gods to discuss a fitting punishment. It was decided that Sekhmet, as a fierce warrior goddess, would be the instrument of Ra's wrath upon humankind.

Transforming into a lioness, Sekhmet descended upon earth, her rage unquenched, bringing with her a bloodlust that was both terrifying and absolute. She began a slaughter, the scope of which was unprecedented, and the rivers ran red with blood. The other gods watched in horror as humanity neared the brink of extinction.

Ra, however, soon realized that his retribution had gone too far. He feared that Sekhmet's rage would leave no humans alive, ending the very existence of the race he had created. But

Sekhmet was in a blood frenzy and would not be easily swayed from her course.

In a desperate bid to stop her, Ra devised a plan. He ordered for a vast quantity of beer to be brewed and dyed red with ochre, resembling blood. This concoction was poured over the fields and around the areas where Sekhmet raged.

When Sekhmet came upon this flooded landscape, she mistook the red beer for blood and, delighted, drank it voraciously. The beer, potent and abundant, eventually intoxicated her. Her lioness form softened, and she transformed back into the goddess Hathor, benevolent and kind, her bloodlust forgotten. The slaughter of mankind was halted, and those who survived rejoiced, praising Ra and Hathor.

The story of Sekhmet and the Destruction of Mankind is a narrative rich in symbolism and meaning. It reflects the ancient Egyptians' understanding of the gods as beings capable of both great wrath and great compassion. Sekhmet's transformation from a ruthless destroyer to a benevolent goddess exemplifies the duality of the Egyptian gods, who could bring both harm and healing.

Conclusion

As we draw the curtains on "Egyptian Mythology: A Collection of the Best Egyptian Myths," we reflect on a journey that has traversed the sands of time, bringing to life the captivating world of ancient Egypt. Through the pages of this book, we have delved into the depths of a civilization's beliefs, exploring the intricate tapestry of gods, goddesses, and mythical beings that form the cornerstone of Egyptian mythology.

We began our exploration with the gods and goddesses in Chapter 1, acquainting ourselves with the powerful deities like Ra, Osiris, Isis, and Set, each embodying different aspects of life, death, and the natural world. In Chapter 2, we ventured beyond the divine to meet other mythological characters such as the enigmatic Sphinx and the chaotic serpent Apep, integral to the Egyptian mythological landscape.

The heart of this collection, however, lies in the myths themselves. In Chapters 3 through 9, we immersed ourselves in the foundational myths of Egyptian culture. From the diverse Egyptian Creation Myths that paint a picture of the universe's origins to the tragic and redemptive tale of Osiris and Set, each story unfolded layers of symbolism and cultural significance.

The Contendings of Horus and Set in Chapter 5 illuminated the complexities of divine politics and familial loyalty. In Chapter 6, we joined Ra on his perilous nightly journey through the underworld, a symbol of renewal and the eternal fight against chaos. The Tale of Two Brothers in Chapter 7 brought us a narrative rich in themes of betrayal, magic, and transformation.

Isis and the Seven Scorpions in Chapter 8 highlighted the dual nature of deities, capable of both protection and vengeance. Lastly, in Chapter 9, the story of Sekhmet and the Destruction of Mankind offered a profound look at the balance of compassion and wrath in the divine realm.

In closing, this book has been more than just a collection of stories; it has been a window into the soul of ancient Egypt. The myths recounted here are timeless tales that speak of universal themes — power, redemption, conflict, and harmony. They are stories that have transcended their origins, continuing to captivate with their complexity and depth.

I hope you have enjoyed this exploration into the world of Egyptian Mythology. If you would like to share your feedback, it is greatly appreciated if you could take a minute to leave us a review on Amazon. It really helps us to continue producing books that readers love!

And finally, if you liked this book, please keep an eye out for the other books in this series, also available for sale on Amazon as well as through many other online retailers. The other books in this series include:

- Roman Mythology: A Collection of the Best Roman Myths
- Norse Mythology: A Collection of the Best Norse Myths
- Greek Mythology: A Collection of the Best Egyptian Myths
- Celtic Mythology: A Collection of the Best Celtic Myths

www.ingramcontent.com/pod-product-compliance
Lightning Source LLC
Chambersburg PA
CBHW071114120626
46546CB00003B/1328